Nature All Around

BIRDS

Written by

PAMELA HICKMAN

Illustrated by

CAROLYN GAVIN

Kids Can Press

For Hayden and Hudson Eady from Aunt Pam — P.H.

*To my family for being patient during busy painting days,
to Karen for pulling it all together in such a delightful way
and to all the birds of the world — you are beautiful — C.G.*

Acknowledgments
*Thank you to Carolyn for her beautiful art and to Kathleen
and the Kids Can Press team for their great support — P.H.*

Text © 2020 Pamela Hickman
Illustrations © 2020 Carolyn Gavin

Kids Can Press gratefully acknowledges the financial support of the Government of Ontario, through Ontario Creates; the Ontario Arts Council; the Canada Council for the Arts; and the Government of Canada for our publishing activity.

Published in Canada and the U.S. by Kids Can Press Ltd.
25 Dockside Drive, Toronto, ON M5A 0B5

Kids Can Press is a Corus Entertainment Inc. company
www.kidscanpress.com

The artwork in this book was rendered in watercolor and gouache.
The text is set in Kepler.

Edited by Katie Scott and Kathleen Keenan
Designed by Karen Powers

Printed and bound in Shenzhen, China, in 3/2020 by C & C Offset

CM 20 0 9 8 7 6 5 4 3 2 1

Library and Archives Canada Cataloguing in Publication

Title: Birds / written by Pamela Hickman ; illustrated by Carolyn Gavin.

Names: Hickman, Pamela, author. | Gavin, Carolyn, illustrator.

Series: Nature all around (Kids Can Press) ; 4.

Description: Series statement: Nature all around ; 4 | Includes index. | Based on content previously published in The kids Canadian bird book (Toronto: Kids Can Press, 1995) and Starting with nature bird book (Toronto: Kids Can Press, 1996).

Identifiers: Canadiana 20190173548 | ISBN 9781771388184 (hardcover)

Subjects: LCSH: Birds — Juvenile literature.

Classification: LCC QL676.2 .H54 2020 | DDC j598 — dc23

Contents

Birds Are All Around

What kinds of birds do you see around you? Do you have a favorite? Maybe it's a heron, a chickadee or a woodpecker. The United States and Canada are home to all these birds and more. Whether you live in the city or the country, you will find plenty of birds to watch and listen to. Birds are an important part of the wildlife food chain, and some animals depend on them for food. Birds also eat many insects that people think of as pests. Some birds carry pollen from flower to flower (called pollination), which helps make seeds so new plants can grow.

In this book, you'll find out more about birds all over, from those you see every day to strange birds, and you'll discover how you can become a bird-watcher. Start your bird-watching adventure by meeting the birds on these pages. They may look very different from one another, but these birds have a lot in common.

Did you know that birds are the only animals with feathers? Find out why feathers are important on pages 8–9.

All birds lay eggs. On page 10, learn about how baby birds hatch from eggs and grow.

Many birds migrate, or travel, long distances in search of food. Turn to pages 16 and 20 to learn why.

Most birds live in nests that they build themselves. See what different nests look like on pages 12–13.

See pages 24–25 to learn how to identify the birds you see in the wild.

Birds Up Close

Birds come in many different shapes, sizes and colors. They may look different from one another, but they all have some features in common. Here are the body parts of a typical adult bird.

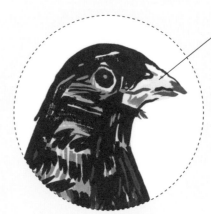

A BEAK is important for grabbing and crunching food.

FEATHERS keep a bird warm and dry and help it fly. They may be specially colored to attract a mate or to help a bird hide from predators or prey.

WINGS help a bird fly. They also help some birds swim underwater.

A bird's TAIL helps it fly and maintain balance while perching. Some tails are shaped or colored to attract a mate.

A bird's FEET may be used for catching food, perching or getting around in its habitat.

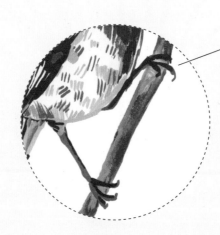

SHARP BEAKS

Many birds have specially shaped beaks to help them eat their preferred foods. These are some common beak shapes.

STRONG AND HOOKED

Birds of prey, such as bald eagles, use their sharp beaks to tear food apart.

THICK AND CONE-SHAPED

A northern cardinal's beak is perfect for crunching and cracking seeds.

LONG AND THIN

A calliope hummingbird pokes its straw-like beak into tubular flowers to reach their nectar.

LONG AND TAPERED

Great blue herons use their strong beaks for spearing fish and frogs in shallow ponds and marshes.

FLAT AND WIDE

Mallards use their broad beaks to strain their food, such as plants and insects, from pond water.

SHORT AND POINTY

A yellow warbler's delicate beak works like a pair of tweezers, picking up tiny insects from leaves and tree trunks.

STRANGE BIRDS

A northern shrike is a robin-sized songbird, but it feeds on small mammals and other birds. It has a sharp, hooked beak, like a bird of prey does, but a shrike's small feet are too weak to hold its food. Instead, shrikes stick their prey on large thorns in trees or shrubs, or on barbed wire, to hold the food steady while they eat.

NORTHERN SHRIKE

Looking at Feathers

Did you know that birds are the only creatures with feathers? A feather may look simple, but no other animal part is as strong, lightweight and flexible. Here are four common kinds of feathers.

SPRUCE GROUSE FEATHER

CONTOUR FEATHERS cover a bird's body and give it shape as well as color. They include the long, stiff flight feathers in the wings and tail.

NORTHERN CARDINAL FEATHER

INDIGO BUNTING FEATHER

FILOPLUMES are hairlike feathers at the base of contour feathers. Scientists think that filoplumes help a bird sense changes in wind and air pressure. They also help contour feathers stay in place.

DOWN FEATHERS are found on all birds. They appear beneath their contour feathers. These special feathers provide extra warmth and help keep waterbirds afloat.

POWDER DOWN FEATHERS are found on herons, bitterns, egrets and parrots. This feather's tip disintegrates into a powdery substance that birds use to clean and waterproof their feathers and keep them in flying shape.

GRACKLE FEATHER

WOOD DUCK FEATHER

GREEN HERON FEATHER

A RAINBOW OF COLORS

Birds come in many different colors, but feathers themselves contain only a few colors. When light falls on a feather, it absorbs some of the colors in the light and reflects others. We see only the reflected colors.

Some birds, such as hummingbirds and starlings, have iridescent feathers that seem to change color as the bird moves. Their special feathers refract, or break, light into a rainbow of colors, like a prism.

RUFOUS HUMMINGBIRD

ATTRACTING A MATE

Male and female birds of the same species may be different colors. Feathers of female birds that nest in the open may be dull colored to hide from predators. But the males of the species tend to be brighter colored to attract a mate. Some male birds, such as goldfinches, grow colorful feathers in spring. Once breeding is over, those feathers are replaced by duller feathers.

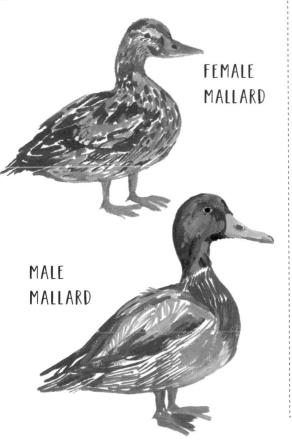

FEMALE MALLARD

MALE MALLARD

STRANGE BIRDS

Unlike most female birds, female phalaropes are larger and more brightly colored than male phalaropes. During mating season, females often pursue and fight over mates. Sometimes, after mating with one mate and laying eggs, a female will mate with other males and lay more eggs in new nests. The males sit on the nests and protect the eggs. At the end of the breeding season, females migrate south, leaving the males to look after the young.

FEMALE RED PHALAROPE

MALE RED PHALAROPE

A Bird's Life

Adult birds begin the cycle again. They find a mate and raise their own young.

EGG

Eggs must be kept warm until they hatch. Usually, the female bird sits on the nest while the male hunts for food. Incubation can take from 11 to 80 days, depending on the type of bird.

HATCHLING

Each baby bird has a sharp knob on its beak, called an egg tooth, to break open its shell. Some birds are naked and helpless when they hatch and have to be kept warm until their first feathers grow.

JUVENILE

At this stage, young birds lose their first feathers and grow longer and stronger flight feathers. These birds can finally fly and feed themselves.

NESTLING

Hungry baby birds stay in the nest and are fed by their parents. Most land birds eat insects, but baby seabirds eat mashed-up fish.

FLEDGLING

When birds grow too big for their nests, it's time to fledge, which means growing flight feathers and learning to fly. Even after a bird leaves the nest, its parents still feed it on the ground for a week or two.

ALL ABOUT EGGS

Birds' eggs come in many different shapes, sizes and colors. The shape and size depend on the environment where the egg is laid and the size of the bird. For example, birds in the auk family lay pear-shaped eggs that won't roll off the cliffs where the birds nest. The color of a well-hidden egg may be bright, such as blue or white, but eggs laid in the open are often dull and dark so they are harder for predators to spot.

Different species of birds lay different numbers of eggs in a year. A pheasant may lay 12 to 15 eggs at once, called a clutch, but an albatross lays just one egg a year. Some species produce a particular number of eggs and then stop, regardless of what happens to the eggs. These birds are called determinate layers. Others, called indeterminate layers, keep on laying eggs, replacing damaged or stolen ones, until the clutch reaches a certain size.

GREAT HORNED OWL EGGS

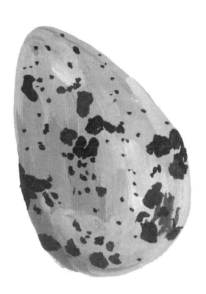

COMMON MURRE EGG

AMERICAN ROBIN EGGS

COMMON NIGHTHAWK EGGS

11

A Bird's Home

Most birds build nests, which are homes for eggs and baby birds. If you were a mother bird, you would nest where your eggs and babies would be safe from danger. Birds build nests in trees and shrubs, on the sides of buildings and cliffs, on the ground and even underground.

BALTIMORE ORIOLES *weave plant fibers, hair and twine into deep, sack-like nests. The nests hang down from high branches in trees and even sway on windy days, like a cradle for baby birds.*

EARED GREBES *build floating nests made of marsh plants in shallow lakes and ponds. The nests are safe from land enemies such as skunks, and the babies can easily go for a swim.*

CHIMNEY SWIFTS *nest in chimneys, of course! A swift uses its saliva to hold its shelflike nest of twigs together and to stick it on to the chimney wall.*

NOT JUST NESTS

Not all birds build nests. Here are some other amazing bird homes.

KILLDEERS *lay between four and six eggs in shallow, sunken areas in open fields. The eggs have brown and black speckles to help them blend in with their surroundings.*

Male and female **BELTED KINGFISHERS** *dig a long burrow high up on the bank of a river, pond or other steep slope. Inside, they dig out a large chamber where five to eight white eggs are laid on the bare soil. Once the babies have fledged, the adults may have a second brood.*

EASTERN SCREECH-OWLS *use hollows in trees and old woodpecker holes for their eggs. They lay two to six white eggs on the debris at the bottom of the hole, which may include wood chips, old feathers and droppings. The parents may return to the same nesting cavity each year.*

STRANGE BIRDS

Cowbirds don't build nests or look after their babies. Instead, the females lay their eggs in the nests of other birds and fly off, leaving strangers to raise the baby cowbirds. Often, the baby cowbirds beat a host's young to food and space in the nest.

BROWN-HEADED COWBIRD

Birds by the Sea

You may be used to seeing birds up in trees, but there are many birds in other habitats, too. Some birds spend their lives out on the ocean and return to land to nest.

The United States and Canada have long coastlines that provide homes for millions of seabirds. These birds are well adapted to their special habitat.

To stay warm in the cold water, WILSON'S PETRELS *have a thick layer of short, fluffy down feathers next to their bodies.*

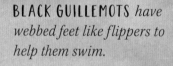

BLACK GUILLEMOTS *have webbed feet like flippers to help them swim.*

ATLANTIC PUFFINS *use their short, narrow wings to swim underwater.*

Like most seabirds, GANNETS nest in huge groups called colonies. They crowd together in nesting areas near good food supplies so more of them can survive.

Like many birds, COMMON TERNS have an oil gland at the base of their tails. When they are preening, or cleaning themselves, the birds spread the oil on their feathers to make them waterproof.

COMMON MURRES have short legs set far back on their bodies, so they walk upright like penguins. Both penguins and murres are expert swimmers, but only murres can fly.

Birds in Spring

Every spring, birds that spend winter in the south return to their northern habitats. Why do they come back? Birds return to the north because there is more food and less competition from other birds there. Many birds lay eggs in spring. They return north to find space for nesting. Smaller birds, such as warblers, usually migrate at night when they are safe from predators. Geese and other large birds travel during the day.

SINGING ALL DAY

You may have listened to a rooster crow at dawn, but have you heard the other birds that sing as the sun is rising? Many birds start the morning with a song and continue singing on and off all day. They use songs to defend their territories and to attract mates. Birds also make different calls when they are angry, frightened or hungry.

In early spring, a male bird claims his breeding territory, the area where he and his mate will nest and raise their young. To keep other male birds away, he perches in high places, such as treetops or rooftops, and sings loudly. The song means "no trespassing." When a female bird is nearby, the male changes his tune to attract her.

MALE EASTERN BLUEBIRD

FEMALE EASTERN BLUEBIRD

NORTHERN
MOCKINGBIRD

17

Birds in Summer

In summer, birds are busy raising their young, finding food and avoiding predators. Some species, such as robins, will nest again after their first family has fledged. Birds are very important to farmers because they eat millions of insect pests and the seeds of weeds that can damage crops. They also eat mosquitoes, blackflies and other nuisance insects.

SPREADING SEEDS

Plants depend on birds, too. Plants use their flowers to make seeds that grow into new plants. Through a process called pollination, birds transfer pollen, a sticky substance, between flowers. When a hummingbird visits a flower to feed on nectar, its feathers pick up pollen grains from the male part of the flower and carry them to the next flower. When the pollen falls on the female part of a flower of the same species, and one of the pollen grains unites with this flower's egg cell, a seed is formed.

Some seeds become part of an edible fruit, such as a cherry or strawberry. Robins and other fruit-eating birds help to spread the seeds around. These birds can't digest the seeds, so they come out in the birds' droppings, often a long way from where the fruit grew.

RUFOUS HUMMINGBIRD

AMERICAN ROBIN

SHEDDING FEATHERS

At least once a year, birds replace all their feathers with new ones. This is called molting, and it usually occurs after the nesting season. Most species lose only one or two feathers at a time so that they can still fly. Ducks, geese and other waterbirds that don't have to fly to catch their food lose more at once. They may be flightless for a short time while their new flight feathers grow in.

CANADA GOOSE

Birds in Fall

As the days get shorter, many birds from northern areas of the United States and Canada head south to find food. Some birds migrate very long distances. Arctic terns are the world's champion long-distance migrants. At the end of summer, they leave their Arctic nesting grounds and head south, all the way to the Antarctic Circle.

MIGRATING FOR FOOD

Migrating birds that feed on insects and flower nectar, such as warblers and hummingbirds, know they will soon have nothing to eat in the winter. Insects will be dead or hibernating, and flowers will be gone, too. Waterbirds also migrate because their food and homes become covered with ice and snow.

Not all migrating birds travel far. Clark's nutcrackers simply leave their rocky mountain home in the fall and head down to the warmer valley for winter. Many birds don't migrate at all. For instance, blue jays remain in the north all year. They feed on seeds in the winter and are a common sight at backyard bird feeders.

TUFTED TITMOUSE

BLUE JAY

BIRD TRACKING

How do scientists find out where birds go during migration? They use geolocators, which are tiny sunlight-intensity recorders with a built-in clock and a memory chip to store data. Geolocators weigh less than 1 g (0.035 oz.), so even small birds can wear them. Based on the sunlight information in the chip, scientists can calculate where the bird is at any given time.

geolocator

PROTHONOTARY WARBLER

Birds in Winter

Have you ever wondered how birds that don't go south keep warm in winter? Birds are experts at winter survival, and they have taught us a lot about fighting the cold. In winter, you might notice that these birds look fatter than usual because they fluff up to trap air in their feathers. The air keeps them warm, acting as insulation. When you wear a puffy down-filled jacket, you are wearing feathers, too — down is really tiny bird feathers.

STAYING WARM

Different birds have different clever ways of staying warm. Some grow up to one thousand extra feathers in winter! A gray jay can puff up to almost three times its normal size. Other birds use one another to stay warm. Chickadees gather in tree holes, huddling together in a group for warmth, while starlings roost together in sheltered areas to share body heat.

Some birds even use snow to keep warm. Ruffed grouse survive cold winter nights by diving into snow banks. The air trapped in the snow is like a blanket, keeping the body heat in and the cold out. Snow buntings, common redpolls and other small birds also shelter under the snow, where they are warm and hidden from predators.

GRAY JAY

WHITE-TAILED PTARMIGAN

WINTER TRICKS

White-tailed ptarmigans have several adaptations, special skills that allow them to survive in their habitat. They live high on mountains in areas with no trees and very cold winters. Ptarmigans turn white before winter to match the snow. This is called camouflage, and it helps them hide from their predators. They even grow extra feathers on their toes that help them walk over the snow without sinking into it. They also save their energy by flying as little as possible.

Beginner Bird-Watching

Wherever you are, you'll find birds to watch. You may see them resting on telephone wires and trees, soaring overhead and swimming or wading in the water. But with close to a thousand different species of birds in the United States and Canada, you may wonder how to tell them apart. These questions and a field guide to birds will help you identify what types of birds you see.

SIZE

• Is the bird small, medium-sized or large?

small

medium

large

SHAPE

• Does the bird have a plump or slender body?

plump   *slender*

SPECIAL BODY PARTS

• What shape is the bird's beak?

strong and hooked   *thick and cone-shaped*   *long and thin*   *long and tapered*   *flat and wide*   *short and pointy*

• Does the bird have long or short legs?

• Is its tail long or short? What shape is it?

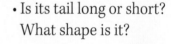

• Are the bird's feet webbed, strong and hooked, or small and weak?

• Is there a crest on its head?

CREST

• What shape are its wings?

elliptical   *thin and pointed*   *long and narrow*   *long and broad*

24

COLORS AND MARKINGS

- What color is the bird?

- Can you see spots or stripes on the bird's breast?

- Does the bird have any patches of color, such as an eye stripe, wing bars or a tail stripe?

BINOCULARS

CAMERA

FIELD GUIDE

BIRDSEED

NOTEBOOK

PENCIL

SONG

- Does the bird's song repeat itself?

- Do the notes go up or down in pitch?

- Does the song get louder or softer toward the end?

- Is the song short or long?

MOVEMENT

- What is the bird doing when you see it?

- Is it swimming, diving or wading in water?

- Is it hopping up a tree or climbing down headfirst?

- Does it glide through the air, hover in one spot or fly up and down like a roller coaster?

LOCATION

- What habitat, such as a forest, lake or meadow, is the bird in?

- What part of the country is it in?

More Strange Birds

EATING ON THE FLY

Magnificent frigate birds never land on water. Instead they fly low and snap up fish near the surface. They also chase gulls and terns to steal their food in flight. The males have amazing red throat pouches that they blow up like a balloon to attract a mate.

MAGNIFICENT
FRIGATE BIRD

AMERICAN
WHITE PELICAN

BIG MOUTH

An American white pelican has an enormous pouch hanging down from its beak. This bird swims around and scoops fish and water into its pouch. Then, it contracts the pouch to push the water out but keep the fish in. Once the pouch is drained, the pelican jerks its head up and the fish slides down its throat.

DRUMMER BOY

Most male birds sing to attract their mate, but male ruffed grouse perform a drum solo instead. They stand on hollow logs in a forest and beat their wings back and forth. The thumping sound starts out low and slow but increases until it sounds like a drumroll.

RUFFED GROUSE

SPOT THE FOOD

An adult herring gull has a bright red spot near the tip of its beak. This spot is a target for baby gulls. When the adult comes back from collecting food, the chicks peck at the red spot. This is a signal for the adult gull to open its mouth and regurgitate its food into the mouths of its babies.

HERRING GULL

WOOD DUCK

READY, SET, JUMP!

A female wood duck lays her eggs in a tree cavity, usually overlooking water, that she lines with her feathers. A day after the ducklings hatch, they climb out of the tree using little claws on their feet. Then they jump down, sometimes falling over 15 m (50 ft.) to the water or ground below without hurting themselves.

WHITE-BREASTED NUTHATCH

HEADFIRST

Many birds sit in trees, but only a nuthatch travels down a tree trunk headfirst. It searches for insects on tree bark. In winter, a nuthatch feeds on seeds, often jamming a seed into a crevice in the bark to hold it steady while it cracks the seed with its pointy beak.

Endangered Birds

Imagine if a bulldozer knocked down your home — you'd have to find somewhere else to live. Many birds have their homes destroyed when forests are cut down, wetlands are drained and grasslands are plowed under for farms, roads and subdivisions. Oil spills, pesticides and other forms of pollution also threaten birds and their habitats.

Habitat loss is endangering some species. When a species is endangered, it means that something is killing it. If it isn't helped, that species may die. When this happens, the species becomes extinct, meaning that it is found nowhere in the world.

All across the United States and Canada, people are working together to save endangered species such as the burrowing owl and piping plover.

Here are some ways you can be a friend to birds, too:

Make a bird feeder and keep it full of food all winter long.

Plant sunflowers, zinnias and other annual flowers in a garden or in pots. These plants produce seeds for birds to eat in the winter.

Build a birdhouse and put it up in early spring before birds start nesting.

Keep birds from crashing into a large window by making a black hawk silhouette from cardboard. Hang it outside the window.

Raise money for conservation groups that protect birds and their habitats.

BURROWING OWL

PIPING PLOVER

MAKE A BIRD FEEDER

You can help birds find food in winter, or at any time of year, by making a bird feeder. Finding food in winter is just as important for birds as staying warm. Food gives birds the energy they need to heat their bodies.

1 Rinse out the bottle. Ask an adult to cut an opening on one side of the bottle, toward the top half, about 7 cm (2 ¾ in.) wide and 10 cm (4 in.) long.

2 With the sharp point of the scissors, carefully poke a hole about 2 cm (¾ in.) below the bottom of the opening. Poke another hole directly across from this one on the other side of the bottle.

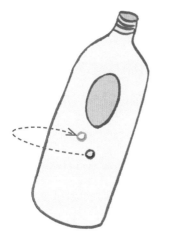

3 Slide your stick into the two holes so that it is balanced in your feeder. Birds will use the stick as a perch.

4 Wrap one end of a piece of wire tightly around the neck of the bottle and tie the other end to a branch of a tree so your feeder hangs freely. Hang your feeder where you can watch it from a window and where you can easily reach it for refilling.

5 Fill the feeder up to the opening with birdseed. A mixture of corn, sunflower seeds, unsalted peanuts and millet will keep every bird happy.

29

Glossary

bird of prey: a bird that catches, kills and feeds on other animals

camouflage: to hide or disguise by blending into the background, usually due to color or shape

clutch: the group of eggs laid by a bird, often all at once

colony: a large group of one or more species of bird that rest or nest close together in a chosen location

contour feathers: long, stiff feathers that form the outer layer on a bird's body and give it shape and color

determinate layer: a bird that lays a limited and predetermined number of eggs in each nesting period, regardless of what happens to the eggs

down feathers: small, fluffy feathers beneath the contour feathers that provide extra warmth

egg tooth: a temporary hard bump on a baby bird's beak or jaw that it uses to break out of its egg

endangered species: a species that will become extinct, or die out completely, if the threats to its survival are not controlled or reversed

extinct: when there are no more of a species left anywhere in the world

filoplumes: hairlike feathers growing at the base of contour feathers

fledge: to grow flight feathers, learn to fly and leave the nest

fledgling: a young bird that has just learned to fly

geolocator: a tiny recorder that scientists attach to an animal to track its location

habitat: the natural environment where an organism lives. It provides shelter, food, water and protection.

hatchling: a bird that has recently come out of its egg

hibernate: to find shelter and become inactive, often during cold or dry weather

incubation: when a parent bird sits on its eggs to keep them warm so they can develop

indeterminate layer: a bird that continues to lay eggs until a certain number has been reached and will replace eggs that are damaged or removed from her nest

iridescent: many different bright colors that change with motion

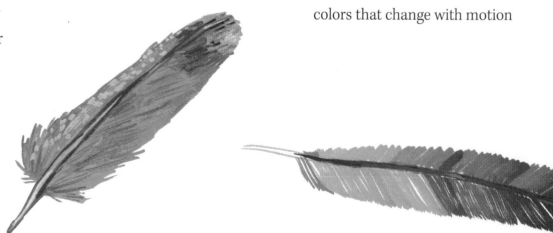

juvenile: a young bird in the process of obtaining its adult feathers and color

life cycle: the stages of an organism's life; for a bird, the stages from egg to adult

migrate: to travel a long distance, usually to find food or breeding territory, or to avoid cold or dry weather

molt: to lose feathers, usually a few at a time, and replace them with new feathers

nestling: a baby bird in a nest that cannot fly yet and is cared for by its parents

pesticide: a chemical used to kill or control an unwanted plant or animal

pollination: the transfer of pollen from the male part of a flower to the female part of the same or a different flower

powder down feathers: tiny feathers that break down into a powdery substance used to clean larger feathers (similar to dry shampoo) and waterproof them

predator: an animal that kills and eats another animal

preen: to clean and arrange the feathers, as well as spread oil from a special gland over them to make them waterproof

prey: an animal that is killed and eaten, usually by another animal

regurgitate: to eat something, partially digest it and then throw it back up. This is how seabirds make their "baby food."

Index